Sizes

Tall and Short

Diane Nieker

www.raintreepublishers.co.uk
Visit our website to find out more information about **Raintree** books.

To order:
☎ Phone 44 (0) 1865 888112
▤ Send a fax to 44 (0) 1865 314091
▢ Visit the Raintree Bookshop at **www.raintreepublishers.co.uk** to browse our catalogue and order online.

First published in Great Britain by Raintree, Halley Court, Jordan Hill, Oxford OX2 8EJ, part of Harcourt Education.
Raintree is a registered trademark of Harcourt Education Ltd.

Editorial: Sarah Shannon and Louise Galpine
Design: Jo Hinton-Malivoire
Picture Research: Natalie Gray and Ginny Stroud-Lewis
Production: Chloe Bloom
Originated by Dot Gradations UK
Printed and bound in China by South China Printing Company

10 digit ISBN 1844 43788 4 (hardback)
13 digit ISBN 978 1844 43788 7 (hardback)
10 09 08 07 06
10 9 8 7 6 5 4 3 2 1
10 digit ISBN 1844 43793 0 (paperback)
13 digit ISBN 978 1844 43793 1 (paperback)
11 10 09 08 07
10 9 8 7 6 5 4 3 2 1

British Library Cataloguing in Publication Data
Nieker, Diane
Tall and Short – (Sizes)
530.8'1

A full catalogue record for this book is available from the British Library.

Acknowledgements
Alamy Images/Big Cheese Photo LLC p. 18; Alamy Images/Pixonnet.com p. 5; Getty/RubberBall Productions pp. 6, 7; Getty Images/The Image Bank pp. 8-9, 10, 12; Getty/Taxi p. 19; Harcourt Education/Trevor Clifford p. 21; Harcourt Education/Tudor Photography pp. 14, 15, 16 (l and r), 17, 20; NHPA p. 13; Robert Harding World Imagery/Getty p. 4; Stone/Getty Images p. 11.

Cover photograph reproduced with permission of Patrick Giardino/Corbis.

Every effort has been made to contact copyright holders of any material reproduced in this book. Any omissions will be rectified in subsequent printings if notice is given to the publishers.

Some words are shown in bold, **like this**. They are explained in the glossary on page 23.

Contents

What does tall mean?

Tall means that something is long from top to bottom.

Most houses are tall.

These trees are very tall.

Who is taller?

These two people are both **tall**.

Who is taller?

The man is taller
than the woman.

Which building is the tallest?

Some buildings are very **tall**.

The tallest building is taller than all of the others.

Can you find the tallest building?

This is the tallest building.

Very tall buildings like this are called **skyscrapers**.

Which is the tallest animal?

Some of these animals are **tall**.

Which animal is the tallest?

The **giraffe** is the tallest animal in the world.

Giraffes eat leaves.

The giraffe is so
tall that it can
reach leaves high
up in the tree.

What does short mean?

Very young children are **short**.

This boy is too short to reach the toy up on the table.

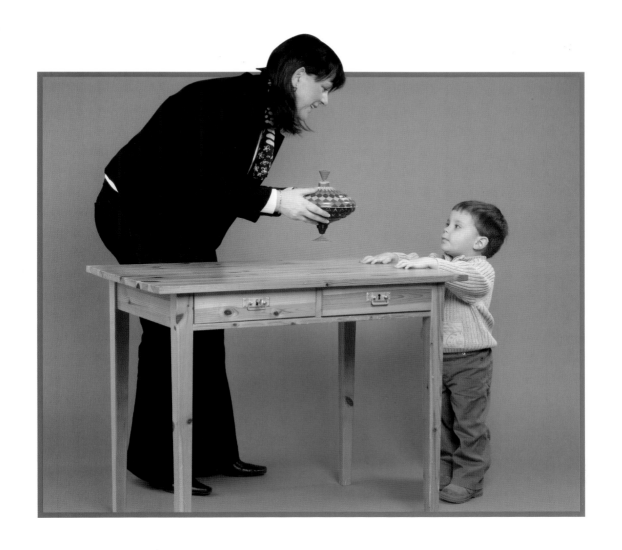

His mother will need to get the
toy for him.

Which is shorter?

The plant with yellow flowers is shorter than the plant with red flowers.

The plant with red flowers is shorter than the plant with white flowers.

The plant with yellow flowers is the shortest.

What does height mean?

When we talk about **short** and **tall** we are talking about height.

These two girls are the same height.

These two boys are the same height.

But the boys are taller than the girls.

How do you find height?

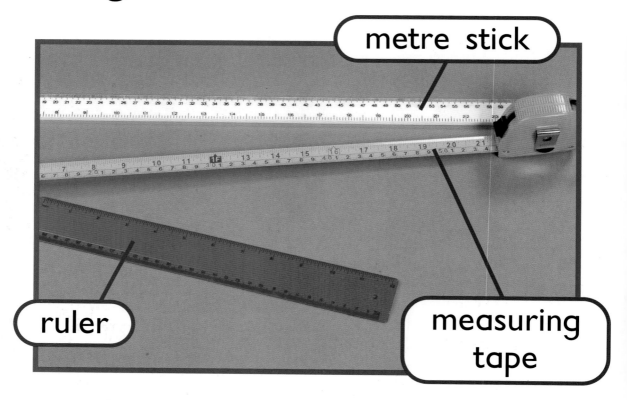

metre stick

ruler

measuring tape

We use rulers, metre sticks, and measuring tapes to measure height.

This boy measures his height to find out how **tall** he is.

Do you know your height?

Quiz: True or False?

1. When we talk about how **tall** something is, we are talking about its height.

2. **Giraffes** are the shortest animals in the world.

3. Rulers and measuring tapes can be used to measure height.

4. Very young children are tall.

Glossary

 **giraffe** animal that has very long legs and a very long neck. The giraffe is the tallest animal in the world.

 **short** not very long from top to bottom

 **skyscraper** very tall building

 **tall** long from top to bottom

Index

Answers to quiz on page 22

1. True

2. False

3. True

4. False

Note to parents and teachers

Reading non-fiction texts for information is an important part of a child's literacy development. Readers can be encouraged to ask simple questions and then use the text to find the answers. Most chapters in this book begin with a question. Read the questions together. Look at the pictures. Talk about what the answer might be. Then read the text to find out if your predictions were correct. To develop readers' enquiry skills, encourage them to think of other questions they might ask about the topic. Discuss where you could find the answers. Assist children in using the contents page, picture glossary, and index to practise research skills and new vocabulary.